BEREAVEABILITY.

BEREAVEABILITY.

SPENDING A LIFETIME AVOIDING
THE REALITY OF YOUR DEATH.

M.J. SZIMANSKI

LIFE IS HARD. THEN YOU DIE.
THEN THEY THROW DIRT IN YOUR FACE.
THEN THE WORMS EAT YOU.

BE GRATEFUL
IT HAPPENS IN THAT ORDER.

~ DAVID GERROLD

TO JO AND ZEKE.
AND JACKI.

🔔 Bereaveability 🔔

Published by SeeSalem
Salem, Massachusetts 01970
www.BereaveItOrNot.com

Cover image: You, eventually.

First published 2013

Manufactured in the United States

ISBN: 978-1-304-73225-5

Library of Congress CIP data applied for.

_____

◣ Bereaveability ◢

TABLE OF CONTENTS

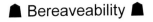 Bereaveability

1. WELCOME

How easy it is for an author to get hung up on the title of a book. And how easily the title can become the toe tag of years of any writing effort.

Perhaps you've read a riveting story on "life's lessons" someone found necessary to foist *en masse, en print,* on an unsuspecting public under the guise of crocheting secrets or corporate success. Everyone is no doubt delighted that the author of the latter was successfully raised by their grandmother in a cardboard box near the airport, but you bought the book to better understand arbitrage.

Or, some foreign airport gift shop/currency exchange of the bodega variety left you with only two choices: a compendium of the author's old, dead Nana's recipes or another's reflections on a riveting life in taxidermy instruction. You leaned toward the the latter since you were assured from reading the back cover that the author really "knew" Lassie. By all means, you passed on the militant mother who launched 600 pages of overly graphic maternal literary salvos upon a well-breeding, if not well-bred, public up to their breast pumps in advice on how everything they are doing is wrong. Bah.

Really, who hasn't been there, if not at such an airport enterprise then at the frightening fork up that limited literary lane?

Should any of these have won a spot on your night stand, it may very well have been because of the book's title.

In that regard, you will find no such ambiguity here.

The title of a book is its Amazon anchor, the word or words used in the very necessary viral support that is word-of-mouth and the brand behind which lies so much time and thought. For a potential reader, the authors hope, seeing a book's title for the first time can parallel the first glance that stimulates a barroom flirtation -- one that leads to a long and fantastic fuck.

This book is called *Bereaveability*. It is a new word, in part, because so many other writers on death killed this author's hope of effectively adapting something refreshing from the more mainstream terms on the topic. The hope is that this title, *Bereaveability*, dangling its dead-center diphthong proudly, will be interpreted as more informative than clever. Death itself is the clever one, something it proves every day. *Bereaveability*, the book, can only to scratch the surface as a cautious and perhaps sometimes comical chronicle.

Bereaveability, the word, has its root in *bereave*, a word that has come to almost universally represent a loss related to death. Yet bereave's roots are actually closer to the more general deprivation of something, to take away. It is used in both ways in this sense and in doing so, accurately conveys the intent of this book. Ability, naturally, defines the capacity to act, to do something -- even if that something is nothing.

This book explores how humans have the extraordinary ability to deprive themselves of serious thought regarding their own approaching deaths. This is achieved through human societal evolution and the inventing and sanctioning the use of ceremony, religion, war, denial, distraction, drugs and a few other mortality-deflecting mores addressed within.

No small part of this is the role played by those who predecease you -- whether you knew them or not. When awareness of someone's death should be triggering a deep, morbid and reflective consciousness of life, mortality and when one's own ship may sink, it seems instead to launch a metaphorical fleet of celebratory lifeboats gleefully boarded by everyone still breathing.

Perhaps *Bereaveability*, the book, will help you understand why in heaven or hell that is.

2. The Scream That Isn't There

I understand death physically, biologically, emotionally, and I believe as well as anyone who can rawly rationalize such things, pragmatically. It is pragmatism, stripped of all else, that gave birth to this book on death.

Yet, where I am lost is how the vast majority of people hurdling toward death effectively elect to fully deny their own -- perceptually, culturally and clinically. It is there, of course, but it seemingly won't affect so many, so many think, for some reason. And, boy, are there some reasons.

Denial of your own death can be dangerous. Or, at the very least, it fosters a lack of preparedness that can blind you to developing a responsible blueprint regarding your handling of your life before it. And for many, how living your life while you have it affects your ranking when you don't, depending on your particular brand of spiritual eternity.

To many, death is like someone watching television while sitting in the direct path of a widely reported tornado. But rather than gather up grandma and Fido and head for the root cellar, they keep changing the channels hoping to find a station where the weather guy is reporting blue skies ahead. Some just unplug the TV altogether.

Television may not yet make such things possible, but the Internet has perfected it.

I have a bit of an ongoing, tech-istential understanding with a friend of mine. As we both consider ourselves grandees of Google, we mutually espouse that any position on any subject can be located and "substantiated." Is Hitler dead? You betcha. Or not. Automobile oil changes at 5,000 or 6,000 miles? Yes. Did the moon landing happen? Please. Will playing the Village People within earshot of your feisty fetus make them gay? Don't be silly. Maybe. Of, course, you unqualified carrier of a blessed event, you. Why do you think they're feisty?!

Delving into death is no different. Look it up. You die. Or you don't. Or your body does, but your soul doesn't. Or, you become a ghost, a guardian angel, a tree, a cow or diaper rash. Never has there been more information available on the subject -- yet most refuse to even consider themselves an object of that subject.

But should everyone go crazy over it? Yes. Why doesn't everyone? Glad you asked. It all goes something like this:

Death is the absolutely worst thing that can happen to you and anyone or anything that you love, and everyone should be screaming at the top of their still operational lungs in fear of it. It ceases all contact with the living immediately, it forces you to look at them devoid of anything that made you love them, and it is the first stage of the physical decomposition of what's left of them. Death is anyone's or any living thing's final act.

Skeptical? Imagine some control group or population such as those living in a village, town, tribe or the world. With that, factor in that they all know and love one special person within that group.

Then, subtract the following: religion and all of its deities, ceremony, and the ability of one person to lie to another -- even "good" lies that are conjured to make someone feel better. There is no booze or drugs, therapy or tobacco, nothing to derail or desensitize the soon-to-be-miserable masses. All that is left are the exposed, virginal human emotions they were born with.

Now, in your mind, kill off that person they all know and love. Leave the body in the town square or somewhere that this population of people can see it. In the case of the world, train a webcam on them. No panning required.

So what would people do? They would become a thunderously vocal, collective raw nerve of agony and anguish, wailing for weeks, wishing to join them -- and sometimes voluntarily do so -- and acting out in ways that attempt to paralyze this mutant growth of emotions repeatedly kicking them in the heart and head.

With no externally induced protective programming, the PR campaigns and codification provided through religion, funerals, other ceremonies, Jim Beam, peyote and Xanax, people experience only the emotions they were born with and by doing so, correctly evaluate the severity and true depth of death.

And here the premise takes a twist. This very natural, horrifying sadness and explosion of related emotions isn't really just about the dead person. It it very much about the realization that you could be next, and there is nothing you can do to stop that, either.

Your predeceased compatriots may be in a better place, but regardless of how many candles you light, who you pray to or what you tell each other, he or she is in the exact same place your mind won't let you acknowledge you're headed if not next, then soon. Refusing to think about it positions you somewhere between being blissfully immortal and riding a Vicodin buzz.

On a milder scale, recall when someone told you they have poison ivy, or they've been in a car accident or are getting a divorce. Now, being completely honest with yourself, doesn't a wave of *whew* come over you that it isn't you? Death brings the same result, only the *whew* is, paradoxically, thunderous yet practically inaudible. You know it's there, what it sounds like and what it means, but you don't feel right allowing yourself to fully, emotionally, guiltlessly bask in its bullet-dodging beauty.

Likely borne of a complex algorithm that no one fully understands, how death affects you is based on some combination of:

- your affection, or lack thereof, for the deceased,
- your own ego,
- your general feelings towards humanity; and
- how generally happy you are, or aren't.

Some degree of what has become the blanket term for anything cerebral not firing properly, mental illness, and apparently affecting everyone to some degree, is probably in there somewhere.

So why subject yourself to the tremendous impact of knowing that you will one day cease to be, have all that you are and done be forgotten by almost everyone, never see anyone or anything you love again and become a helpless mass of biological goo good for little more than fertilizing ferns? All of this is so horrifying a thought that people have evolved a series of protective mechanisms to force it into subconscious remission.

And when, over the eons, the true realizations of the nasty finalities of death began to stir in cultures and cliques about to the point of discussion, but not quite; a new religion, ceremony and/or range of post-death/spiritual survivor solutions are introduced to a freshly-torn-off-scab of people. An opportunity for forced assimilation is recognized, and an opiate is offered to and willingly toked by a fearful populace.

Over history, and still operating with feckless abandon, the Grand Poobahs of their respective tribes knew that not only do lives paralyzed by grief and fear not survive, they're all a bit too wound up to build bridges, fight in wars, pay taxes and otherwise serve said Poobahs. And just as bad, they're damn embarrassing. Who wants to rule a sad and whiney people?

So, let's kill a couple of birds with one stone, they surmised. The death-dreading delirious are told that if they stop their sniveling, there's a BIG SURPRISE waiting for them when they do die. Ta-Dah! They won't die. Well, not really. They get to live their lives all over again, sort of, in a better place with everyone they know who died before them, playing harps on clouds, singing at Carnegie Hall, with virgins, at 22-years-old again, but without acne, or all of the above. What a deal!

Basically, the mastery over any such group is possible if their fear is identified and insulated through some sort of doctrine of distraction. All the better if the population is made to feel better through that insulation and distracted to the point that they don't know it's a distraction.

Those immune to or without time for being de-griefed through group hugs or through any sort of soul-saving structure in such calls to calm are the self-subjugated: *The Inevitablists.*

The Inevitablists boldly and bravely acknowledge that their terminal Timex is ticking. Most of *The Inevitablists* have wills, many have grave sites, paid in full, and all are no fun at parties. They're a bit too seemingly realistic, followers of an orthodoxy of pragmatism that is so matter-of-fact it closes the door too quickly on the true depth of their pending demise.

They acknowledge that death happens, while magnanimously including themselves, but they do it with the gargantuan gusto of slamming the buzzer on a game show.

By taking the bullet so blindly, bravely, they're dodging the impact it has on the metaphorically miserable skin, sinew and bone it tears through on its way to proving them right. In so antiseptically offering themselves up as the target they acknowledge they are, they're espousing, yet underestimating, the biological inevitability while their tomb-deaf alter ego is sticking its fingers in its ears and clucking non-senseisms to drown out anything like to reveal further, gory details.

The Inevitablists have taken denial to such an art form that they, somewhat ironically, qualify themselves for grand marshal status in the Denial of Death parade. There they are, waving confidently before the crowds of their simpatico brethren the *Pseudo-Eternalists*, those who are pretty damn sure they're not going to die at all, while seated in black tails or tiara, or both, on the back of an antique hearse right behind the Shriners and the Budweiser Clydesdales. (Although, in the interest of full disclosure, the latter two attractions are traditionally hired for such events and not necessarily high deniers themselves.)

Regardless, *The Inevitablists* inevitably doth project too much about being fine being dead. Perhaps this particular cushion is stuffed with their need to be right more than having to explain that they've given it very little thought at all. Denial comes in many forms and has been around as long as mankind. Admit it.

Managing Mortality

The combined theological and secular moral-boosting mortality books about death's effect on the living, laid back-to-back, could get you to hell and back. From sensitive, coddling, gingerly crafted language intended to buffer the loss, to the suck-it-up-they-wouldn't-want- you-to-be-miserable sort of literary, toughish love chest thumping that nourishes, not without its bruises, the self-help set.

And then there are the lesser lessons of those post-terminal tomes that usually fall somewhere in between. "They're in a better place." and "Live your life, bake a cake!" illustrate just a wee corner of the "managing your mental view on mortality" industry, and business is just fine.

Born and bred over the millennia was the multicultural, geographically limitless, even pre-Internet, idolistic intervening in the form of prothlesizing PR campaigns that the lemming leadership decided was necessary in order to keep their furry flocks from going crazy over death. No doubt held in various 2nd century and later then venue versions of Ramadas, the *Statement of Purpose* agenda item that cauterizes and kicks off such convenings was clear. Somewhere during these aristocratic offensives in mind-control maneuvers between SWOT and Group Morale, they wisely adopted *noblesse oblige* as a license to mangle lesser minds into *foie gras*. In other words, English, by manipulating the minds of the masses that they desire dwell under their spell, they pretty much convince them that they're doing it for their own good. *Sainte merde!*

Think about it. Why do the vast majority worship? Yes, there is no doubt a need for a spiritual fulfillment in many or most intent on steering clear of that heathenistic isle of Atheism. But being something of a visual-proof-seeking sort of species, even those outside of Missouri, spiritual need needs to be something they think they can see, ideally above – and by doing so, and it being there, to them, look up to.

After all, if said humans, especially those carrying that nasty Genesis gene of Original Sin, are going to drastically alter their lifestyles while living in order to invest in a life that may be better and longer later, they want to be damned sure they're in charge of their own potential damnation -- or at least have a say in any plea bargains before their final celestial sentencing.

All so fascinating, really, how the mind which controls the body permits itself to be controlled by this general, and sometimes generic, need for spiritual fulfillment. And why might the mightiest of men and women cave with such unbridled acquiescence? If you said fear of death, you are correct. If you said to make death more, um, palatable, you are also correct. Hell, death is beyond palatable in some radically drawn quarters. In others, it's more desirable than life with more points scored for taking as many others with them as they can. Most, however, prefer to wait it out, hoping against, or ignoring that prospect that, they will ultimately be the cowering coyote under the Acme anvil.

Since humans first started accidentally cutting themselves on Stone Age implements, often with terminal results, or waking up next to sex partners who stopped moving and started decomposing, man realized they were finding themselves at the mercy of something that could take away not only who and what they wanted to keep, but also themselves.

The astounding irony of looking for something larger and mysterious in control over this, overhead, cannot be ignored when one considers the possible causes of ancient death beyond hunting accidents, chariot duels, coliseum cage matches and war. No, often something much, much smaller than themselves was mysteriously and effectively killing themselves.

Disease, parasites, genetic time bombs, cancer, stress over a bad hunt and the incalculable afflictions that worked themselves from the inside out would probably have been more terrifying than that time Theonius the Unlucky was hit by a meteor fragment while plowing another farmer's wife. (Karma FTW!)

The human mind was developing, and reluctantly grasping, another brand of fear and confusion, a no-doubt disappointing development during an era of emotional angst thought quelled by the acceptance of the power of the constellations and paying homage to the seasonal Corn God.

Humans were subject to the mysteries and terrors of the unknown such as the remarkable, fascinating powers of the volcano and the vagina. And while floating alone in the universe, albeit *en masse*, death pounced upon them for sea trials. Perhaps death even spurred the development of certain emotions in the yet-to-be-fully developed humanoid brains carried around on the necks of human ancestors. What better synaptic catalyst for denial? That tool with which one thinks, can shut itself down, for good.

Even if death as the biological end then was understood as that, something especially difficult to ignore in the warmer climates or during the summer months elsewhere, there was more than enough feverish and often pungently-propagated fear for the survivors to stew in their own confusion, frustration and what came to be know as loss and sorrow.

These increasingly unjustified attacks on pretty much everyone over the generations began mentally metastasizing in the minds of a people formerly simply happy to have enough to eat and the occasional roll on the bearskin rug. Having everyone they know eventually yet inevitably drop like flies, and then drawing drawing them, no doubt helped then spur the blame, anger and the rest of the stages of what was to become the foundation for the steps of grief as employed to this very day.

So people learned to sit on their sadness by shifting their position about death as their ultimate destination, or at least picture it more like a travel brochure for Trinidad and Tobego, and/or begrudgingly acknowledged that it was OK. It simply became easier to fear, blame, worship and generally concoct something to ignore or accept those unknown entities so determined to tirelessly reduce their races.

Yet, it is important to remember that denying death evolved as much as a result of showing strength as supplanting sadness. As mankind became cockier, tribes became armies and armies became city-states and city-states became countries, or something like that. And with that meteoric rise in machismo, the boo-hoo of a lost belle, beaux or bro became bad news on a more threatening level. Shedding tears showed weakness and lack of control. Quivering quivers and trembling tridents hardly instilled confidence. Yet thankfully, during this transition, there was still some degree of human empathy since everyone knew they were borrowing some version of the same time. So various, perhaps even unspoken semi-truces chimed in despite trends and orders to exact terror otherwise, and few vulnerable victims were heartlessly bludgeoned while blubbering about their Bubbies.

3. COUNTING

Everyone should take the time to use the Internet access of their choice to look up "worldwide deaths by cause." A fun read it isn't, but plan to be enlightened for as long as you're around to digest it.

As with most reported statistics representing a moving target such as propagating and perishing people, it takes a few years to keep check of drifting decimal points and strive to insure fair representation of who made the list by gender and age; whether it was through malady, murder or something else and where they spent their time on Earth.

With all of that assumed to be trustworthy and in place, the World Health Organization (WHO), one of the reliable stewards of such happy thoughts, estimates that, roughly and for example, approximately 58,000,000 people died in 2005. Even if you can get your head around such wiggle room catch phrases as "reporting countries" and any advisory asterisks, assume for this exercise they may have erred, if at all, on the side of caution.

So, that's 58,000,000 people! What's probably most astounding about that number is that you weren't one of them. Really, what are the odds -- a question that based on your unlikely desire to know makes statisticians suddenly sexy.

The year 2005 is cited here simply because it offers a relatively recent and credible, albeit antiseptically tagged, *Mortality Index*. Although 2005 brought Katrina, an earthquake in Pakistan, the bombings in London and some other deviousness and disasters, each year brings its own similarly thorough and high-volume wave of expirants. Pick a year, any year, and you will find similarly nasty, widely cast death nets.

Now, having survived the years since, and long enough to read how lucky you are, know that death's lottery still considers you a ticket. Such reliable rankings allow for a solid 150,000 human deaths a day, so you won't always be dodging that bullet or brain tumor, heart attack, car accident, incurable infection or freak accidental slip on the wet floor of a Piggly Wiggly perhaps, ultimately, dying of embarrassment.

If you do dwell on the specific statistical realities that apply to you, and you run into your bookie or some Washington, DC poll-meister fluent in the oddities of odds (or someone, enterprisingly, perpetrating both), don't bring them up. Once they assess your prognosis, which ironically, is also theirs -- albeit *in admission absentia*, you risk condemning all within earshot to life awash in hand sanitizer for having gone near you. This, to be followed unjustly just for speaking the truth, by other unbearable injustices such as a mortal semi-eternity of never being joined on a golf course during even the slightest threat of a thunderstorm. Basically, they'll think you're depressed or pathetic, or that you read this book, all not necessarily mutually exclusive.

Yet in all of this, despite how granularly you examine how this may all apply to the still-living you, don't lose sight of the size of the overall crop being so grimly reapered. Had every last one of the now-not-here in any given year been active participants in the Facebook cult, for example, their mass demise would barely put a dent into its purported monthly LOL-Fest of over one billion acolytes. Perspective can be fun.

Here's to tomorrow's 150,000. Duck!

4. The Afterdeath

The term "afterlife" has a decidedly upbeat ring to it. It doesn't make the person any less dead, but it seems to give them more of a fighting chance should there be something else out, or up, there.

But really, couldn't the term "afterdeath" also apply? In the interest of chronological accuracy, shouldn't it?

Technically, it's the more current condition of the two. And the refreshing honoring of more dead-on vocabulary following a death might be more welcomed given the prevailing technical numbspeak by the the medical, morgue and funeral home cadre of cadaveresque-leaning linguists. It is interesting how many ways there are to say someone has died without using the word dead.

Afterdeath, or it could be said anything not resembling the Kleenex/tissue genericism of afterlife, may, like a metaphorical autopsy, cut a bit too close to the bone. More often used split in two, perhaps *after death* more closely and too graphically attaches itself to the degradation of the physical body -- something people really go out of their way to avoid thinking about. Whatever the reasons, the died-in-the-wool afterlifers would blanch at the blasphemous bandying about of such a truculent term.

And, there have been no centuries-long rehearsals about what to say of an afterdeath when asked by a child or non-denominationally inclined neighbor or coworker -- although some seem universally prepared. "What happens after death, Mommy?" the inquisitive spawn from a House of Agnosticism innocently inquires. "Why worms, dear. But we all know worms are beneficial." the dutiful mother then replies, believing that her beliefs are the best beliefs to be believed. Here, theological non-committal meets science meets, maybe, reincar-something.

Well, everyone knows worms are good.

Regardless of whether you call it afterlife or afterdeath, death really can't be termed a loss if it is indeed this temporary. It's more of an eternal condition of metaphysical meandering. "Oh, I was so sorry to hear about your loss," is one of the many common niceties that not only avoids using the word death but somehow, also, pseudo-sympathetically translates your wife of 50 years into an inanimate object." The afterdeathers would immediately snap back: "Oh, Myrtle isn't a loss dear, she's theologically misplaced."

And then it becomes confusing.

The dead may or may not know:

A) if they're dead,
B) where they're headed or, frankly;
C) anything at all. They may be at a loss and/or lost, but there's only one shot in three that they **are** a loss.

If they are indeed headed somewhere, the reality of their redirection explodes exponentially since they may end up anywhere, including but not limited to:

A) At the Right Hand of a god,
B) In hell, so **not** at the Right Hand of a god
C) Awaiting the resurrection of one or more deities they may or may not have worshiped in life (how potentially embarrassing...and, literally, damning).
D) As a barn owl or a dandelion or fecal parasite (Karma's a bitch.)
E) Other

Anyway, afterdeath just never won any etymological adoration, possibly due to its negatively connotative cousins: aftermarket, aftershock and afterbirth.

To that add that afterlife not only had a longer brand presence, its marketing was nothing less than a couple of thousand years of masterful. And the other one made people say that "death" word.

So, this terminal, terminological trajectory shoots you from life to death to afterlife and wherever the afterlife goes, if it indeed ever starts. Yet with that, are you any more impervious to worms? Or do they matter less because by having an after-belief, and the prayerful support of others dedicated to orating that after-belief in unison -- all while casting fetching upward glances -- you are insured a spot on an eternity-junket more supreme and less susceptible to any decomposition of the soul?

Do thousands of like minds liking the same liturgical lingo influence what might be left of you spiritually the way rural townsfolk have been known to successfully supplicate to have Little Timmy ascend injury-free from the well? Well?

But here's the real question: In the grand volley of one's deftness in dodging death's drill call, what role does what one calls death play? And remember, this isn't going to always be just about the other person. Everyone's in this draft.

Apparently, plenty. Afterlife glides off of the tongue like "New and Improved," yet somehow, before it leaves, reverse physics apply, and it is simultaneously swallowed hook, line and sinker. It's such a necessary bi-sayable noun in this tangle, being both a place and a thing, that etymological evolution has fused it to too many parts of the brain to safely lobotomize it without an embolismic exorcism. Life without an afterlife, and certainly without an afterdeath, would be, well, lifelackluster. If the dead can think so, they would certainly, or do, agree.

And for once, this applies to many beliefs and types of beliefs. Not only do arkfuls of major, "recognized" religions sanctimoniously sanction afterlife, but afterlife is also employed by those who's employment depends on its existence and what it purports to offer. Psychic insighters rank it equal to or above their polished lucite balls and gloss-black manicures.

And lest we forget the medical practitioners who, curiously but somehow seemingly continuously, find themselves in the secular/sentimental/self-preservationist position of endorsing the afterlife phenomenon.

On those occasions, physicians may dubiously offer supporting testimony to patients who slipped in and out of mortality and approached the "white light" shone upon them as a result of the former's surgical blunders. What better, hopeful and non-lab-tested testimony when coming uncomfortably close to otherwise taking responsibility for pushing the limits of the terms of their malpractice insurance policies? A more enlightened medical community is all everyone ever wanted.

And although under normal circumstances a misty-eyed scalpel wielder would at best be disconcerting, those doctors who place themselves in this position somehow appear almost formidable and seem to take some pride in their role as the shedders of such sympathetic tears.

So, with a confused but enlightened recovering cardiac patient and their confirmed vision of a celestial, beaming doorway leading to cushions of clouds and WAV-quality harp beats, another book is co-ghostly-written and another talk show slot is filled. Yet, more importantly, acknowledgment of a possible error in surgical judgment and potential lawsuit is avoided. Publicly feigning ignorance on eternity is far less humbling and a more legally sound defense strategy than being dragged through a deposition in front of an AMA stormtrooper with a box full of medical records and five courtroom rows of anxious heirs.

So, at the point when a cold self-assessment of one's medical career determines it is hanging by a suture, going on the talk show circuit to speak and tweak with the celestial and/or the scientific in this regard is necessary and *de rigueur*. Since you weren't actually there, you can't say where the white light would have come from or gone to. But, you can rest assured that it will dim before prismatically bending into a pesky, career-ending spotlight and beam upon your boat slip.

5. THE FUNERAL SHOW:

The Hearse You Came in On

The Funeral Show is beyond complex. It's more of a mournsterbating multiplex attended by the still living determined to witness someone they know dead still. After the death-ed event, so begins a cross-country cortege, comprised of all walks of life and acquaintance, dispatching themselves to the dais of their newly departed.

But why do so many come from so far and wide to see someone dead who, in many cases, they wouldn't have made half the effort when that someone was still someone? The answer is simple: to make sure they're dead. Sure, that can sound cynical, and technically clinical, but it's true. More than one religion and many schools of grief-counseling agree.

Closure, as it's called, is the balm to calm those left behind with the troublesome burden of being alive. Anyone left bereft by death, since they first heard the news by text while chasing a blowing plastic bag across their lawn or undertaking some other critical mortal endeavor, feels a range of foreign emotions from a hole in their heart to grief in their groin.

Ultimately it hurts, or at least feels uncomfortable enough that an emotional eruption of some sort feels necessary. With such sadness swelling in the bereaved, a ceremony was created that allows them to relieve themselves in public. This display has become known as the funeral.

As with any theologically trans-engendered person, place or thing assigned a higher power and purpose by those intent in their attempts to worship it, the final idols take different forms to suit their sinners. The ceremonies are also bespoke by belief but, as a rule, all still deal with the physical and attempted emotional disposal of the dead.

Whether they're sailed off on a Viking dingy, fried on a funeral pyre or in an undertaker's oven, or sent the more traditional six feet under, there is finally one, common, belief that all religions share: Don't leave the dead lying around too long. In that regard, the postmortem procedures are pretty much the same but their names are changed to reflect the congregant. You say potato.

Before such a cast off, cadaver-honoring participants and parishioners awkwardly ogle the expired's eternally fixed face. This is the result of what the undertakers undertook to recreate on someone they've never met while it was still operational. A face, often, that well-meaning widows, widowers and other lovers and loved ones help permanently and often unrecognizably helped mold through their unintentional insincerity.

Tapping on their own, unique experiences fitting out a Colonial club basement or redesigning their own resemblance through plastic surgery, these next-of-kin-commissioned cosmetic creations are often based on photographs older than those used on many a coital-cruising personals site. My, but how fetching Sheila
was in 1951!

Perhaps visually perpetrating the past on the passed allows the loved ones to better remember the former in their finest fettle. Or, rigor mortis reacts with ego and guides the grief stricken in a fight for the fabulous -- Over my dead body am I going to have everyone think I was married to someone who looks like a corpse! You've got an airbrush, use it!

Yet, they should be indulged. Theirs are the most connected and relevant memories. If they want to try to peel back time on someone who has none left, let them. And should there be gilded gates in heaven or the inclination of the deceased to rejuvenate and revisit through an orgasm of ectoplasm into a ghostly or another, other-worldly figure -- and encounter the equivalent of a reflection -- only the most sensitive to the spirit world will hear them wail "*Who the hell is that!?*"

Closure is something of an all-encompassing term weaved to drape over that which comprises the ceremony and stunts meant to blunt death's blow. Closure is about tightly caulking the drafty door in your mind that allows the cool, cruel breezes of memories and sorrow continue, for too long, to chill you to your bones. Closure doesn't exactly produce a warm fuzzy, but if properly executed and absorbed, more the fuzzifying of otherwise bald and barren heart-wrenching reactions. For many, especially those who appreciate and possess the domestic and creative wherewithal to craft their own sympathy cards, it's a good thing.

Absolutely critical to opening yourself to closure requires a careful and comfortable understanding and acceptance of the funeral. Whether it drowns you in dirges, manifests itself as a standing-room-only (except the corpse, of course) booze-soaked wake or blows into a dubiously legal spreading-of-ashes over the sand pails and sunburned on a public beach, the funeral is literally the last rite of passage. And given the gravest possible condition of the guest of honor, it is easy to assume that anything else would, and should, make you feel more grateful to be alive.

As you wallow in the windowless funeral home viewing rooms with ceiling moldings three feet deep, over drywall, and the almost completely successful sensory expungement of formaldehyde from the basement, you realize you are strutting on death's catwalk. And class act that you are, you feel compelled to comply with the earthly etiquette of the dead.

For women, black hats if in a Societal spotlight, but at least black suits, dresses and shoes worn, perhaps for the only time, out of respect rather than to perpetuate the illusion of smaller feet. Men in blackish to grey-leaning suits given spousal dispensation to smoke cigarettes, outside.

Dress darkly and clam up. Better yet, look clammy. Emulate your host. Imitation as the sincerest form of flattery transcends through to death, at least for as long as you can see the emulatee. Sartorial homage is paid to the host's somber shades of darkness, making he or she the least lively of the party the fashion leader -- usually for the one and only time in their existence. Yes, wear a pallor in the parlor. Now that's the new black!

Admittedly, any gathering involving the presence of a dead person before the event even starts is bound to be a downer.

However, this makes it easier for everyone to fit in since the behavioral burden is defined by what you shouldn't do.

Execute occasional and barely audible murmuring while eye-dabbing -- regardless of actual tear duct production. The need to reek of respect compels you from inducing regurgitation of the new jokes you feigned offense to at work, and thus, half of your small-talk repertoire. Instead, use universally accepted, library-quiet enunciations consisting of benign banter not dissimilar to the ripples almost heard immediately before the first gong at a seance. Children at a minimum. Visions of Miller Lite, martinis or magnums to be swilled in sadness later, at a maximum. Hell, of course we're going to their house after, how often do we get a sitter? You're driving!

Yet what really happens during those viewings and wakes and the sittings of shiva is often more than etiquette and the compliance to customs. The funeral becomes a party that is party to a paradigm shift of anthropologic significance. Somehow, being more like the dead descends upon the living and isn't lifted until the ceremonial rattling of cocktails at the after-party.

Then, at the gathering's grimmest, the spiritual leadership present offers fantastic and usually uplifting descriptions of how the departed are actually eternalish now and undertaking interplanetary entertainments appropriate to their sins and station. A communal sigh of sorts evacuates if not from the lungs and lips, then the hearts and minds of the bereaved believers, and somehow, these rites seem all right.

And there are those who take this a step further. Can it be, or is it, more than that? Those of the Voodoo Higher Priest hierarchy along with professional ESPers and hallowed Halloweeners claim special knowledge of when and where to pierce the thinnest veil between the living and the dead. And their ways may work, too. But are funerals the true forum?

Perhaps funerals are the fidgeting finger barely plugging the leaky dike of death. The somber payings of respect, New Orleans notwithstanding, that cosmically emails invitations to those who predeceased the currently deceased. There they all are, just on the other side of the folding wall dividing the funeral home's French Provincial furniture from the complimentary and convenient coffee station kitchen annexed by the chronic chatterers. Are they really there? Do you care? Would seeing them be in any way more effective in making you consider your own demise more than a fresh-ish body in an open casket?

What will it take if not the face-to-face of a funeral to convince you how close you are to being a lying down stand-in for the next one, to be the royal ringmaster at the next cadaverly coronation? How do sportsmen assume immunity to the annual bolts of late summer, golf course lightening that reduces foursomes to threesomes, or a sassy stingray that's hell-bent on skewering their SCUBA gear? How does everyone immunize themselves from thoughts of their own demise if not hypodermically, then hypocritically?

No, you don't think of your own bright lights in tunnels dark even when seeing a dead uncle three feet from your nose as you kneel before him in that eternally uncomfortable one-sided conversation. And under what delusion do you feel you can legitimately and indefinitely avoid placing yourself in their place? Easy. It's not about you this time. The plastic letters on

the hallway sign directing you there from the parking lot, the snappy obit, the silk banners on the preposterously large flower arrangements, resembling nothing from nature, on leggy stands like drag queen sentries guarding the gone. Could such subliminal visions trigger long-dead, disco-ish, only-in-your-head tunes such as *I Will Survive*, yet played, for the sake of propriety, on an accordion?

No, you have it writing, and in silk yet, that it's about the them who now aren't. It was their time. They are out of their misery. They lived a life good. Goodbye or even good riddance. Naturally, try to stay on the high road and avoid going too far with anything resembling "I'm better than you, you're deader than me." Karma has been known to attend and attend to such affairs, sometimes swiftly.

Yes! You made it through another one, a funeral that isn't yours. Thank God it's November. Cool enough to send your eerie ensembles back into the closet, with your denial, rather than to the dry cleaners to be injected with, ironically, their own concoction of formaldehyde. No sweat.

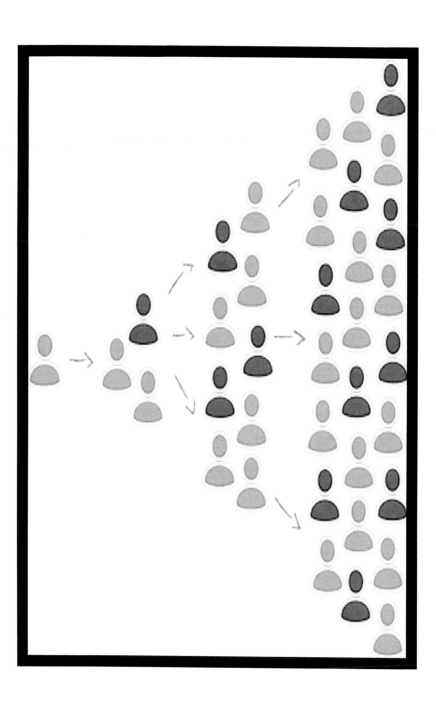

6. It's a Social Media Mourning, Everyone!

"Have you heard?! Cousin Bill died. So young. With THAT FAMILY. Those LITTLE GIRLS!"

"Why, yes of course there's a Facebook page. And you can sign the guestbook at the funeral home and on WhyDidHeHaveToDieSoYoung.com and InstantOrphans.com Oh, and buy one of those flickering candle things. They're cheap, and they take Paypal! Remember when we used to spend all of that money ON FLOWERS!"

"My, and the tweets are so sad, they break my heart. And his bowling/work/sex/hemorrhoid/antique car adventures on the Web...Who knew?! I had no idea he was so complex, but isn't that always the way. You don't really get to know someone until they're dead and you WANT to find out about them. And, of course, they can't take down all of their Internet stuff now, can they? Yea, get to it when you can."

And with that, a question. How does more people knowing of a death faster through what is now the human, God-given-right of an Internet connection affect the impact of a death or deaths upon the cyber savvy survivors?

And does the reality that you are one of the aggregate mob of those knowing faster, albeit through a laptop or an iPhone, cushion the blow? That is, knowing everyone else you know also knows virally, versus a teary-eyed spouse, partner, mother, father, sister, brother, parole officer or AA sponsor spreading the dreaded word to you directly by phone or what used to be called face-to-face?

First, admit it. Although your grief may be numbingly and fetal-position-inducingly sincere, you know you want to know who doesn't yet know. So that you can tell them. You've been insanely jealous and in your mind, justifiably pissed, of the Internet since it revealed where you found your "great grandmother's" borsch recipe or outed your all-star high school quarterback son.

And notifying others of the existence of news that someone they know is no longer in existence is a bit of a sick service, really, but one that you justify as a public service. Never is there a better opportunity to gear up and launch your own Shock and Awe campaign and show that Internet who's got the goods. Aunt Trudy will be first, you think, as the widow/widower/child/sibling/creepy osteopath blubbers into your shoulder.

And since such a human visit from the first-string griever is giving every indication that they are employing, at least in part, the archaic approach to personally passing on word of the passed away, how do you know if Aunt Trudy, and the list of others now uncontrollably and exponentially growing in your head, know? Easily enough done, and executing it bathes you in the light of empathetic munificence. Simply ask: "How is everyone taking it?" to which the only plausible response is a list of those who know and those who don't. Do try to resist yelling "Bingo!" You know you can begin to keep score when your company is gone.

Yet however true, that is all a digression.

In facing death, do you feel better or worse learning online about the death of someone you know and/or love? Does it matter? If it does, why?

Here is one argument for the "it feels better" side:

The Internet antiseptically delivers much of what you call upon it to offer -- or that which it foists upon you if you aren't careful about which cookies you keep in its jar.

In part, this is because, *obviously*, what you are really seeing is only two-dimensional and *isn't really there with you.* You are not in Rome actually eating an artichoke. Or dipping your dog in a flea bath. Or making a soy burrito. Or perhaps most to your dismay, in the room with a lesbian threesome and a well-hung midget acting surprised when a transexual fire brigade shows up and joins them. You are insulated. It's less real because it is not only not there with you, its source is usually far away and you can, theoretically, control when and whether or not you want to experience it. All of that, and you're only wearing your underwear.

You are old enough to remember how news of death was conveyed before the Internet. And, gosh darn it, in some ways you miss that. That face-to-face or phone-to-phone immediacy that exposes you not knowing what to say about the deceased. That hypocritical gnawing that strains your ability to withhold what you know you had better not say about the deceased. Those exercises of actual, real-time interaction that you feel you must endure in order to truly feel the loss, or *be there* for the person and in some way shoulder some of it with them. Or, at the very least, fold whatever genuine sorrow there might be into the guilt of knowing you can always say, "Yes, I heard it directly from them. I'll never forget where I was that day." With such pain you endure, it's almost difficult to feel more sorry for the deceased.

So, yes, there has never been a better way to communicate the death of a loved one. And never have there been such immediate and comprehensive ways to access news of a death in your life. And in sharing that, why phone when you can email, text or reach practically anyone through their online personality dumps? Spic-and-span.

Before all of this rabid interconnectedness, you had your pockets of privacy and the luxury of choosing which doors, when knocked upon, not to answer. Even if your curtains moved, it was still plausible you weren't home. Then doors, and the walls that held them, crumbled somewhat slowly in the beginning. Early email did get lost or junked more aggressively, and there were fewer cyber cabals through which to congregate. When the effort then was to find others you know or knew or who were of like types, the challenge now, should one dare to dream it, is to find at least a kilobyte of anonymity.

Impossible, really, and really, it's your own fault. By buying into what you thought was a better and more efficient way to interact, you have carved the metaphorical equivalent of your non-published phone number into the roach-ridden walls holding up the busiest outbound prison pay phones in the U.S. penal system.

And with the loss of privacy and the gates that guarded you, came Nigerian scam artists, erectile dysfunction drugs, or any kind of drugs for that matter, instant "guaranteed" loans and intrusive, penetrating, thrusts climaxing with news of death.

Death, that equal opportunity deployer, is now closer than you ever imagined. It can easily find its way into your inbox, Twitter feed or cell phone during Junior's tuba recital, uninvited, with a cortege of hapless hyperlinks to the gory details about someone you didn't know you no longer know.

For many, thumbs will continue to be a blur spreading news on all manner of hey-didn't-you-know-this-deceased-so-and-so? Yet for others, that is all just pixelated impropriety or a quandary. If you could, should you block "dead" from your inbound everything as you may be doing with your emotions? If you do, don't do it for yourself, since if you're next in such a text, you're unlikely to be surprised by the news.

Regardless, now might be a good time to clean up the far reaches of your cyber-presence since selectively or cumulatively, yet not always objectively, it is bound to become your online epitaph. Do it while you can.

Ironically, the less you leave there, the more your mourners will be forced to actually remember you as you were here.

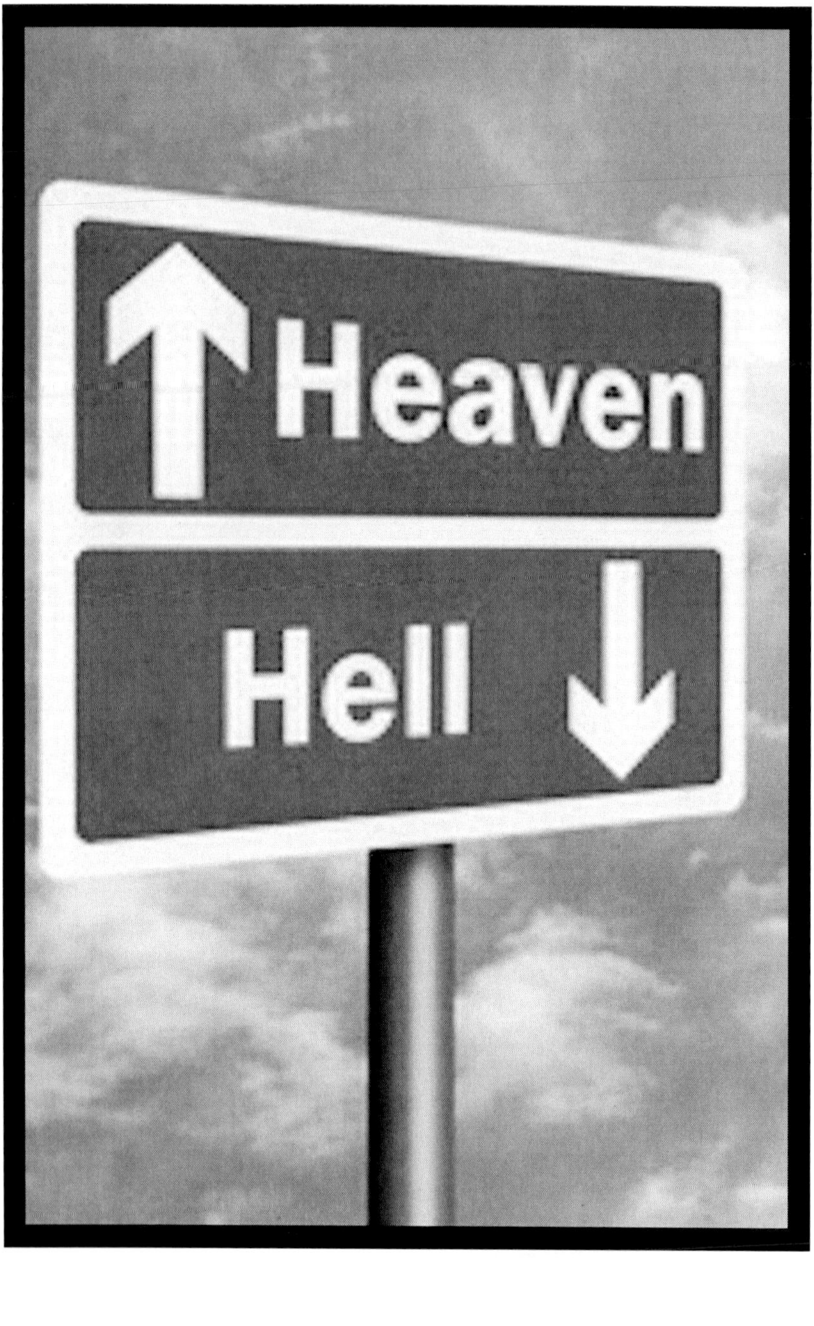
Heaven
Hell

7. Demographics and Damnation Death Digest

Lot in Life	Religious Roulette	Eternal Infernal Interpretation
Why you think you matter.	How your interpretation of the rules of your ruling deity affect your quality of afterlife.	How you envision hell.
Wealthy	Whether WASP or just the WAS, tithing through your CPA or tipping at the tabernacle buys you solace and slumber. Crush the competitor, and keep your money in off-shore Edens, because employing many, regardless of whether it's through your own enterprises or generationally transient stock ownership, is looking out for one's fellow man, isn't it?	I say I'll be fine, but if everyone's going to be nude down there, I'm a bit worried about my small penis. Don't we get a cape or a pitchfork or something?
Middle Class	Church is for Christmas, Easter and funerals or, should your deities differ, their non-Catechismic cousins, unless you have a bag on. And you know, from experience, that being so bloodshot within earshot of hymns and homilies isn't going to be good for anyone. The magnitude of your suffering swells exponentially should ambient aromas of incense and formaldehyde snake up your schnoz.	Nervous, but with a closing argument to play out as follows: "I tried to be a good husband and father, Lord. Can I help it if my freak, queer son decides to take up hairdressing and tree hugging? No! Not my fault. Right?! I KNEW it was his mother! And those magazines I hid, and that thing with that hottie at work, I just thought that was you testing me and you expected me to fail to prove I was human and not as good as you. That's all in the Bible, ain't it?"

Demographics and Damnation Death Digest

Lot in Life	Religious Roulette	Eternal Infernal Interpretation
Why you think you matter.	How your interpretation of the rules of your ruling deity affect your quality of afterlife.	How you envision hell.
Poor	Whatever God wants, God gets! When I can. But I can't always. Because I'm poor. It's God's fault, but not really...It's his plan (or something). I sing my ass off in the pew though, I know He's gotta hear me. And I can't even read music good!	"Oh, HELL no, I'm not GOING THERE! Why the hell should I? I've had it HERE! Have you seen where I live? What I eat? Who I know? Good god, God, you want to talk Eternity, how about that lottery line at the Citgo? I've HAD my eternity!"
Faux Pious	Do as I say, not as I do. Oh, and I say what you should do pretty well. Which sort of makes you think I do it, too. But I don't.	I believe that my salvation will come vicariously through those to whom I've preached to because I'm so eloquent-like, and I've read most of the Bible. I don't actually follow everything it says because, frankly, it's too much for one person. And God Himself said that He won't give us more than we can bear. I think that's that golden eighth commandment or something around there. I also leave Biblical passages instead of tips in restaurants.

Demographics and Damnation Death Digest		
Lot in Life	**Religious Roulette**	**Eternal Infernal Interpretation**
Why you think you matter.	How your interpretation of the rules of your ruling deity affect your quality of afterlife.	How you envision hell.
Batshit Crazy	God tries to tell me what to do, I think, but there's a lot going on up there, and by the time I get most of it sorted out, my Thorazine kicks in.	Well, here's the problem with that...If I go to hell, won't the demons in my head technically be home, and then they can leave and run off to their little demon families down the way? I think that would be worth it. I could have more time to myself to track down those @!$#%&!@ black helicopters chasing me all the time. Hey, can they even fly down there? Sweet!
Republican	I'm doing GOD's WORK. He'd be a fool to touch me.	Yea, well, that God's work thing didn't always work out. That's gotta get me some points down there, right?
Democrat	I'm doing God's work for God's people who, on occasion, may not necessarily WANT to work. But that's OK.	I have never been more unsure of anything in my life. Is not having a backbone overlooked there, too?

Demographics and Damnation Death Digest

Lot in Life	Religious Roulette	Eternal Infernal Interpretation
Why you think you matter.	How your interpretation of the rules of your ruling deity affect your quality of afterlife.	How you envision hell.
Independent	Of course I believe in God. But His omniscience from up there doesn't always seem to be as powerful as nonniscience down here. The less I know and the less I decide, the better off and more popular I am. You can have the cerebral heavy lifting, God. I'm good.	Agnostic. (Naturally.)
Religious Radical	"I WILL KILL FOR YOU!" "OK? We good? That thing you wrote that that guy at that holy place I went to said that you wrote says so." "I WILL KILL FOR YOU!"	Pretty sure knowing about hell isn't going to be necessary. Arranged with his buddies to pack his rectum full of C-4 and wire his corpse with a detonator for the ride just in case. It goes off if he heads anywhere hotter than 450 F.
Hypocrites	Do as I say, not as I do. But not like the Faux Pious. Hypocrites seem to be less aware of the contradictions of their thoughts and actions, making the sale all the more convincing and the damage all the more severe. Treacherous through unacknowledged denial.	Feel safe but not smart enough to really think it through. And they often also have a small penis, but their intellectual capacity is even smaller. And THAT'S small.

8. To Hell, You Say?

It is morbidly and cartographically convenient that hell is said to be below. With that plot point established, we can add a metaphorical gravitational pull to all of the other factions and factors, real or imagineered, that are said to help propel these immortal human morsels in its direction. Go south, yon sinner! It's only natural!

Although human strategies for dealing with the inevitability of a hell are probably endless in their approach and execution, a few stand out. Keep in mind that one has to generally believe in hell in order to muster up enough enthusiasm to formulate a plan to avoid it. Or, at least believe in it enough to concoct and sock away a backup plan should   dark whispers of the possibility of hell begin to reveal its existence.

For many, any unidentified fear can be hell. And since a brush with death begets fear as sure as Aram begat Aminadab, such a brush is, for many, too close a trip toward hell's mothership.

Yet, it is all so cocooned in conjecture. Hell is apparently a super-secret club that conventional wisdom and Hollywood portray, and some would say the latter operates, like some gangs and branches of organized crime. Membership is a privilege -- and permanent. Leaving is not an option.

And hell, if it exists, only seems to appear really, really postmortem whereas entering what is interpreted as heaven includes enough of a liberal leave policy to occasionally permit a visitor-member passage back to mortality. That procedure isn't entirely understood, despite the millions of words espoused on the issue, but it usually involves:

A) **Floating above the operating room table.** (Note: If you are thinking you might die soon, or anyway, have an operation. The operating room ceiling seems to be the on-ramp.)

B) **Being at peace and floating while wearing a hospital gown.** This may seem an impossible task since it is likely very difficult to be at peace in a garment seemingly engineered to demonstrate its sartorial flaws, under such conditions, by flapping your genitalia in the ethereal breeze. Screw eternal bliss, pray for cloud cover.

C) **White-Light-At-The-End-Of-A-Tunnel.** Frankly, a light of some sort seems to be a prerequisite in revealing that you are even in a tunnel. Otherwise it could just as easily be a big, dark, opaque hamster exercise ball or cosmic coffin or some shipping apparatus. But maybe that's the point. White, as a rule, does project all of the correct, heavenly, undefiled connotations. Everyone knows black lights are most likely lining hell's runway. And strobes risk setting off involuntary epilepticism or causing certain Baby Boomers flashbacks to too-favorable, erotic memories and the accompanying woodies and wetness all while in that gravity-defying, gap-filled gown. Yea, sorry. You can't unread that.

Now, back on course. As you approach said light, should it not be your time for some reason, and depending upon the breadth of your religious beliefs, you will usually get close enough to see your Uncle Joe and Aunt Helen and possibly Patches your first dog -- who, by the way, is SUPPOSED to be on a farm -- and someone that looks or feels like an authority figure.

He, She or It is probably also the one denying you entry. Perhaps there's a dress code, and you're not dead enough to know it. Or perhaps you have some unfulfilled "mission" back among the unambiguously living. Or, just as likely, your surgeon finally noticed that an Altoid that fell out of his mouth and is lying on your spleen, and they are hell-bent on removing it and its minty goodness.

The point is, taxiing untimely into such a heavenly experience occasionally sends people, or whatever they are during the process, back.

The other direction.

However, the involuntary booking of such a passage to what is considered hell, if only because it's not heaven, offers much less in the way of documentation. Even the most progressive otherworldly bookstores and websites are mysteriously lacking in such soul-sucking, subterranean sojourns from those purporting to have made such a visit with proof of reentry, unreported, immortal illegal immigration notwithstanding. No, it seems like a straight drop. Bloop. Ouch. Hot. Eternal damnation. Damn!

Even if given the opportunity, it's unlikely backpedaling into your mortal coil to reassess matters when approaching a hellish eternity is an option. "Please, go ahead, I don't want to hold you fine folks up. I'll catch the next ferry, for sure. My, the Styx is choppy today!" By then, it's either too late or there's credence in some of that Eastern Religion-based processing procedure that transforms you into that miserable and mute lower life form you apparently deserve to be. Either way, you're never heard from again until, or if, you master the ectoplasmic exercise of hurling a marble ash tray at your widow as she pegs away at the Craigslist posting to sell your treasured 1966 Mustang.

But despair not! You would be hard-pressed to find a religion, or a house in New England for that matter, that doesn't feature a mention of dalliances if not with the devil, then with his devilish devotees.

For many, getting too close to the fire of hell and its hellions is akin to sin. Apparently, sin is something humans cannot do on their own without prodding. And hell's occupants -- or perhaps even transients -- are the Catacomb Catalysts, a name worthy of a 4.0 GPA biker gang.

If this is true, then there is something of a way out, yet still not a way back. From an adolescent breaking a lamp in the living room playing the known-to-be-forbidden game of indoor football; to those intent on butchering brothel types; to gun-toting, and firing, road-rage-ridden Los Angelenos, blame is often directed to nefarious outside influences. Whether this strategy is an attempt at karmic recompense or legal self-defense, the hooves leaving tracks in the mud leaving the scene are usually just footed by scapegoats.

In all that has been written over the centuries in Biblical texts, holy scripture of any sort and by all of the other religions and their sects on stones, in scrolls and on skins, how fitting it would be for humans to have as their clearest, most succinct and most consistent spokes-god be Flip Wilson. After all, wasn't he the Hemingway of hell with "The devil made me do it?"

Telling someone "May your soul be in heaven an hour before the devil knows you're dead" may be a polite gesture, but it is hardly likely. As far away as everyone thinks hell is, it is still too close. If indeed sin is spurred by hell's expatriates, then it, and they, may be literally right under your feet.

And the next time you hear someone idiomatically offer that they have been "to hell and back" in describing a mugging or marriage, double check with them to determine if they were in any way being literal. The chances are slim, but following every potential lead is necessary to get to the bottom of this.

If you are not unabashedly the sinful sort, generate an unholy amount of unfulfilled good intentions. Hell is supposed to be paved with them. And if you become a top producer, it would be difficult to imagine you wouldn't get word that a highway had been named in your honor.

9. SUICIDE: TAKING THE SELF-INFLICTION EXPRESS

Planning Your Own Dietinerary.

Admittedly, addressing suicide can be a poison pill when purportedly supporting a premise on the human denial of death. Yet, as plain as the body of a successful self-succumber outlined in a mélange of police chalk and plasma, here it is.

And although almost universally societally inappropriate, suicide is welcome here as an area of discussion due to the paradox it perpetrates: Those who decide on suicide qualify as potential deniers of death's durability because many may be driven by the blinding need to leave the living more than being part and parcel with the departed. In other words, rather than worshiping death, thereby obviously demonstrating a belief in it, they buy into its plausibility since they do not deem living a viable option. To those of a certain generation, it's like giving up that new avocado kitchen for Door Number 3 and know that you are stuck with whatever's there.

Suicide, as a cause of a cause of death, can also be a tough pill to swallow for the survivors. It is, in a quantitative emotional sense, likely to more deeply and dastardly affect a greater number of others known to the self-deceased then, say, usually involuntary causes such as falling into a volcano during a Hawaiian honeymoon or choking on an avocado pit.

And unless you were present at an episode involving the latter, but absent knowledge of Mr. Heimlich's maneuver, suicide tends to inject even the most tenuously-connected survivors with a much higher dose of guilt. That is, versus natural causes, however unnatural or even unintentionally hilarious they may be.

Having known someone who would rather talk to no one forever than ever talk to you again can be confusing. Given the chance, many tell themselves, perhaps I could have helped. Possibly true. But planning an itinerary for eternity tends to be shrouded in secrecy. And unless you unmask, confront and turn them around early enough in the process, you may only be left with diving under them before they hit the sidewalk. That seldom ends well for anyone involved.

When assessing if someone is considering their own assassination, you must also be willing to, metaphorically, take your own bullet should you misfire. This potential miscall can manifest itself in embarrassment for one or both of you, trigger a dramatic affront and heel digging fueled by an honest denial, or a lie, cause other outraged offense or save a life.

Whatever goes on in the minds of those who choose to take their own lives is probably nothing short of angst in the aggregate. And you may very well be a contributing part of that aggregate through various sizable contributions to said accumulated angst.

In other words, and depending on the relative clarity of thought by the suicidee leading up to their fatal *fait accompli*, you may have been a factor in the no-win slalom ending with that fatality. Unfortunately, specific details about whether you were a contributing cause, or cause for one of the regrets warmly and genuinely felt during the waning life of the now lifeless, are bound to remain eternally sketchy.

Yet should you be burdened with playing the role of the non-cadaver in this bleak business, know that the unknown doesn't come without plausible, if not tangible, options:

• *Knowing you wasn't enough*
• *Knowing you was too much*
• *Knowing you didn't matter; or*
• *Knowing you prolonged their life beyond when they might have previously planned to end it.*

What you can know for sure is that you're unlikely to never really know. Suicide has been called selfish. This would be an argument for that.

The reasons for suicide are as diverse as the methods. Most people can never fully grasp the cerebral calamity that not only causes the brain to execute itself -- but allows the brain to allow it to happen. It is possible the Edsel felt and mechanically reacted the same way. A sort of self-fulfilling prophecy where operational imperfection begets the need for internal termination. Of course, mutant strains have evolved offering inexplicable immunity to some resilient human subspecies such as politicians and plutocrats, but the sheer number of suicides outside of those generally disturbing demographics seems to demonstrate this: Introspection into one's perceived imperfections can indeed trigger the need to trigger the deed.

In many cases, you and everyone else known to the no longer were part of a tally along with other human and non-human factors -- each with varying degrees of value. It is the sum of this tally, weighed against the sum of the perceived benefits of suicide, that matters. Yet the concoction of this value system, and the individuals' value of the results of that value system, are not by any means exclusive to suicide.

Behold and be aware of the more vapid applications. On a much lesser scale, you may use such ambiguous arithmetic to assess, say, the importance of your presence at a party or company picnic. In evaluating whether or not to go, your intellectual abacus beads off the factors that calculate the short and long-term ramifications of your decision. Who will you offend? Who didn't come to your party? Joe owes you money, and he'll be there. Here's my chance to snatch Laura's recipe for rhubarb rugula or that extra Xanax lying forgotten in her medicine cabinet. Eh, but I have to stop and get gas, and it's raining like out of the Bible...screw it.

All of that in just a fraction of a nanosecond. Hell, who hasn't been there...and not gone because they've been there?

And although everyone has the capacity to tally fro and to, some seem only capable of using such analyses for matters related to living life -- while others are prone to and/or programmed by genetic gerry-rigging that allows the score they tabulate to end it.

In this matter, those who feel that segregation is far in our past should consider that potential suiciders, and those who purport to never make it part of any inner dialogue, are as different as black and white. And as in many such societal divisions, one group resents the other for either its perceived failings or its perceived, and unfair, benefits. To which group you assign the highest value pretty much determines which team you're on.

There usually isn't any middle ground such as *suicide curious*, unless, of course, it's just a phase and you were drunk. Yet, a sloppy cynic might classify non-suicide lifer types along with those who never experimented sexually in college, inhaled, or considered going from neocon to Green -- or vice versa.

And occasionally whining "I could have killed myself" for the shallow sartorial sin of underdressing for some country club clambake doesn't count unless you at least tried and blood was drawn or pharmaceutically potent vomit visible.

No, many of those who enjoy living are content to keep doing so until they die at the hand of God or a handgun. They also obviously seem to be the majority -- a statement evidenced by the burgeoning human population. Of course, rather than the possibility of an overwhelming human preponderance for giving living a tally high, the human species may suffer from wide-spread genetic ineptitude with respect to its self-annihilation. It is likely that those of you with hopes and dreams for your loved ones and humanity back such an optimistic horse.

Perhaps genes know better than to bundle themselves into anything that resembles turf that is the least bit chromocidal. They seek better neighborhoods inclined to age gracefully and have a more stable reproductive value. Eons of human self-preservation bred a self-defense mechanism that can usually be relied upon to prevent placing a shotgun in your mouth or blowing out a pilot light for your own selfish purposes. The former can be more aesthetically devastating than over-tagging a Banksy, and the latter, with one ill-timed flick of a Bic from the chain-smoking cat lady next door, risks a blow up job no one enjoys.

Perhaps it's even mitochondrial, and somehow internally audible, as this brand of maternal DNA thunders inside of the cells passed down to you screaming: "Don't run with that knife! And fergodssake, don't run yourself through with it, either!"

Regardless, the presence of suicidal successes reminds everyone of the ultimate control they have over their own deadly destiny. At any time, anywhere, for any reason, you can end it all. Feeling down? Then down you go! Who doesn't love a jumper?

Suicide has even been known to be emotionally contagious: The long-term spouse who can't live alone, the parents suffering agonizing guilt, the fanatical music groupie who's obsession hurled himself off of a cliff in his Lamborghini while texting his dealer. He was going to text me next! I just know it!

Perhaps for some, suicide is like heading toward a door that opens to an unknown destination in a crowded theater during a fire. Whatever is on the other side of that door is way better than being in a crowded theater during a fire, right? Even if that door happens to be on the building's third floor, leads directly outside and is in a building that had its fire escape removed 30 years ago. All you can think about is the fresh air going down. Try to be upbeat. Given the mess you're likely to leave behind, you'll want to remember yourself that way.

And whether or not you've accepted that you, and everyone, is destined for the fatalistic footsie that rewards all players with a spot on the slab of fame and wearing their finest post-autopsic toetaggery, know that what that morbid medal says about you may be a more permanent legacy than your suicide note. This is especially true if said tag includes a police case number -- something sometimes omitted when natural causes are presumed to prevail. Killing oneself is, after all, illegal in the eyes of many who make mortal laws and immoral in the eyes of many who make moral judgments.

With respect to where in hell any spiritually immortal innards might be headed, the act is also sometimes theologically classified as "self murder." Etymologically that sounds less selfish. But again, it is anything but. Your fatal foray falls into that theological loophole that is homicide. You killed, dammit. And this time, we're not talking about your three nuns on a Vespa on their way to vespers joke at your sister's wedding. This is serious!

Above all else, the suicide of someone you know may most effectively open the door to at least some narrow admission of the existence of you own mortality. And frankly, that's what this is all about. The twist here is that such clarity gains dubious purchase in your head through someone, now no one, who was generally considered to have a twisted mind. The inmates running this particular asylum not only took the keys, but they've taken big swathes of your clarity on such matters. Are you so capable? Can you stay in the theater?

Being situated near the self-extinguished fuels the awareness of how death is so close, so ready, so yours for the asking or taking. Yet, if not of that on-the-brink breed of those who are also destined for self-extinction, it is easy, and perhaps natural, to consider them not like you but a departing breed apart. One who is planning their own dietinerary is, in a very real sense, feeling a particularly insidious case of bereavement now. To them, perhaps, they are here but already gone, and is the here part that's the problem.

Is there really a difference between seeking death's lodging because the brochure seems to offer all of the incomparably appealing amenities you feel you need and leaving the living because you feel as if you've overstayed your welcome?

They are not the same.

10. THE TURDS AND THE BEES

A bird shits on your car. Dammit!

One hundred birds shit on your damn car. Dammit! Dammit! Dammit! Dammit! Dammit!

But that felonious, fecal flock offers a better story at the carwash, or with your shrink or possibly even your insurance company.

Admit it, despite the potential for greater damage to your paint job, the exponentially greater dump of excrement can also inflate the event's overall societal importance. Being a prize dumpee raises one's social profile in certain circles, whether those not revolving within them outwardly admit it or not.

Such scatological horror can become a sanctimonious honor. You deserve it, being shit upon most of your life. Now, you not only have proof that your failures are not all your own, you get a ripple of recognition for it with one, coordinated, bowel-blasting bonanza. But as you ride through the carwash for the ninth time, and despite the accolades from your barroom and bowling brethren, you secretly hope this is the climax of it all and less combative skies will prevail both over your car and over you.

All soon to be relevant, and an awkward and perhaps crude introduction, so this example is offered:

You read about some allergically-inclined guy, EpiPen-less, being stung by a bee, and he dies. Damn! I hope he didn't have a family. (Some would also extend that sympathy to the bee.)

Then, you read about some guy running over an underground bees' nest to "teach'em a lesson about screwing with my lawn," and he's stung 1000 times and dies. Ha. Sucker.

Both men died. Both responses are realistic. But doesn't the latter example sort of take the emotional and sympathetic sting out of the end result which, after all, is the same? And if that's true, how noteworthy that the death deemed more deserved was also much more horrific. Nice species, you.

All of this is a demonstration of man's ability to, at will, eschew basic sympathy, religious regulatory reminders and anything loosely classified as humanitarianism. From those simple seeds sown by the latter example's collapse of compassion, is the potential for mustering raw hatred of someone they do not even know. And this new, nameless nemesis, this heretofore unknown victim of their ire, now, at the very least, falls logically and categorically into their minds as Those Who Deserve Death. A classification that can expand a bit too easily to include in-laws and that bitch receptionist at work.

But this entire internal evolution and experience also does this: It brings them one step closer to death themselves, but as an antagonist -- for a change. Admit it or like it or not, they've approved the bandying about and use of death. They've brandished it as a weapon, a tool. They have, perhaps you have, partnered with it if only for this sole purpose, now. And in some remarkably twisted and human way, they have diminished death as a real fear or threat to themselves because they've taken a voluntary ownership of it before it takes an involuntary ownership of them. Very ballsy, empowering, hot.

Perhaps the best analogy is, not inappropriately, a military one: germ warfare. Those contagions humans were raised to fear and scrub or medicate away became allies in the war against, whatever. What you knew not to go near is now being bred and launched against others with deadly intent by, perhaps, a militaristic you.

So even if you don't wish death on those whom you are now able to consider deserving, signing off on its general use and approval, in some cases, to dispatch them to it is just as bad, isn't it? By aborting your sympathy with what you think may just be a nod and a wink, you're metaphorically mailing them Christmas cards full of anthrax. It's a slippery slope.

And then there's this: The impact you feel for what you consider those unjustifiably unfair events happening to you diminishes with the impact of something you deem as bad happening to those you deem due. At least in your mind. And that's where it counts, right? Ideally, this is someone you're not too crazy about, or like the guy intentionally running over the bees' nest, just, to you, crazy. Either way, you care less if your life is bad as long as there is regular evidence that someone else's is worse. You ride to victory brandishing your proudly unsheathed *schadenfreude*. After all, you were on the other end of this, and 100 feathered behinds, only recently.

It's sinister how gratifying it all might become, and equally twisted how your internal manifesto begins to materialize and grant you a sort of self-immunity, or at least a long-overdue sense of balance, from future karmic persecution.

Slippery, indeed.

11. Vanquished Valor

One of mankind's greatest if misguided gifts to mankind is passing on propaganda on how passing on isn't so bad. This postmortem presumption may be, for many, the foundation of any fear about your own death that that is lacking, missing or mummified into remission.

How are humans qualified to give afterlife advice as if it were on sexual, teenage base-running, when no one with any credibility can speak of their own, lasting backseat romp with the Grim Reaper? This is essentially like non-members of a certain club telling other non-members of that certain club how bad that certain club isn't. Everyone is worse off for the premature passing of Abbott and Costello and what they could have done with that. Who's on first, indeed.

Forgetting your own death for a moment, which this author hopes shouldn't be too difficult since that is more/less the premise of this book, consider how death keeps showing up in your life and how it affects everyone except you. It seems to be everywhere: the Internet, television, radio and what's left of print media. Death is like Oprah, but nowhere nearly as popular in many markets.

Death also seems inextricably affixed to practically every important issue before the living, and politicians. With such high stakes for humans, pretty much everyone has some sort of opinion about death's role and its consequences. Death provides the reason for, and divisiveness over, health care, abortion, gun control, Social Security, global warming, safe sex and many operas. And in typical, arrogant human fashion, those passionate about such political plums wield death through words, worship and the wills of gods like they have control over it.

This phenomenon is at its worst when executed with grim *gestalt* for war.

War breeds death in such unimaginable numbers that the tally can overwhelm the terror and makes those witness to it dumb numb. Worse, war justifies death in ways that, if opposed, can call your patriotism and loyalty to your communal good into question. War blows. The warlords know it, and people know it. Yet warlords and people keep serving it up and oh, how death eats it up. War: It's what's for death's dinner.

At its peaks in popularity, war's attraction incites more recruitment than riots. Being a warrior, whether pot-scrubbing private or genocidal general, gives license to use force to protect one's home turf; defend a flag and a philosophy; ram the right religion down heathen throats, or just kill them; win the heart of a ladylove, or her brother; or simply insure three squares, a reliable haberdasher, barber and free travel.

Wagers of war and their fife-and-drum publicists push their death messaging after something of a religious model, but in reverse. Somewhat astoundingly, that seems to work, too. War seems to be immune to conventional wisdom.

With many religions, the mortal mark is duped into denial of death's dark details through time-share sales pitch eloquently espousing how they should pay now for a more secure and pleasant eternity later. Wall-to-wall carpeting included.

In war, glory is often best achieved through gore. No one in uniform working the cash register at the PX ever had their statue erected in the town square, regardless of their rank. Those immortalized in marble were so reverently chiseled for painting foreign towns red, as long as it was with someone, anyone, else's blood.

Corpse for corpse, contemporary wars have many a current contagion beat. With modern medicine holding back the Grim Reaper strain-by-strain, war also has a deadlock on frequency and duration.

Skeptical? Worldwide, list all of the new high-profile diseases that have surfaced since, say, 1900. Now, list all of the wars. Triple bonus points if a war caused a disease. Notsomany diseases cause wars, however, at least exclusively. Usually such causes fall under oil, ego, religious fervor and real estate.

Perhaps similarly recent natural disasters run a close second. Yet, in some cases, their threat has tumbled since such survivalist solutions as Doppler Radar and the advent of duct tape -- a diligent duo serving to safeguard the furious flying glass from Boca condos. Still, sadly, tsunamis still plague the planet seemingly more than the plague. Some tradeoff.

The point here is that there are fewer natural or manmade death-in-your-face body counts than the cumulative carnage of war. War is the full f-ing package: frequency, ferocity and finality with the biggest numbers in the hitman parade.

Does enlisting in the military immediately preceding or during a war provide evidence of patriotic tendencies or those more suicidal? If the latter, how the former so generously greases the skids to send you there.

War can make death right. War provides you with the human extinguishing equivalent of a handicapped parking pass that gives you a big, close spot nearest death's front door. Worse, you're promoted to the role of death's barker at that door. Step right up, folks! No bothersome fire department capacity limits, and no waiting!

Sure, on the surface, war is nothing but bloodshed and destruction and, well, death. The latter being rather difficult to dispute as casualties and iPhone cameras increasingly converge in the same scenes of slaughter.

But the full disclosure of those indisputable highlights has never stopped a war from being funded or manned. Some military marketing magicians even use such ceremonial carnage as selling points to increase enlistment.

Firing the human carnal desire to be knighted by the war lords *du jour* with your own *007 License to Kill*. Feeling low on that whole carnal desire thing, no problem. You could be gleefully slaughtering scores of total strangers to protect your family, your country, your way of life. It's your duty, dammit!

So while your most animally active temporal lobes are licking up the delicious flavors of death and destruction slathered over them, such as the rat-a-tat-tat rationale for being a recruitee, its gun-toting gooeyness inextricably sinks in, binding to your constitutional and Constitutional-defending fiber.

There it nestles, perhaps next to the parts of the Bible you remember because they-are-the-ones-God-REALLY-meant, are other, related transmogrifications that now make up your new spiritual you. War helps you storm troop over anything resembling the Golden Rule. *Thou shalt not kill* now wields an asterisk like armor. And after all, didn't your deity also have the wisdom to bestow upon man, you, the AK-47 and the M1 Abrams Tank?

Is war a religion? Maybe. Serving in one is not dissimilar to worship, although a bit in the do-as-I-pray-not-as-I-do Conquistadoric sense. Rather than pledging your soul, though, you're a G.I. Joe putting your entire human shell in one hand-grenade-heavy hand basket. You are the General Issue that the military high priests own from the minute you are baptized at bootcamp when they shave your head and size you up for non-civvy skivvies. Talk about a draft.

Making the case for death = war is like shooting fish in a foxhole. But there is the undeniable social aspect that death in war can not only make you dead, it can make you popular -- even in posthumous posterity.

It is reasonable to believe that men and women enter into the military service for their causes and countries for a variety of reasons. Whether here or there, or whether reacting to glowing recruitment statistics or abhorrent reports of children forced to hold rifles too criminally soon after pacifiers, the reasons for becoming part of military might also often depends on how much death's blow is cushioned with ticker tape. For those riding shotgun with the pretty girl in the open car driving down Main Street, death has never existed less.

Anyway, everyone seems to be primed for a fight, anytime, anywhere. Countries, semi-countries, UN-unrecognized groups of people who went to all the trouble of having some fabulous new flag designed or view themselves as both smart and threatening for wearing the same hats, possessors of plateaux they swear to God, God swears are theirs, all tend to get testy when tested.

12. Vampires Suck

Yes, everyone is aware of this in the most Nosferaturistic sense of the word. But if modern technology combined with piss-poor economies has demonstrated anything, it is that English is a living language. It is in the availing themselves of that etymological flexibility that power and utility companies channeled hip, at the expense of one particular branch of the walking dead, by branding them with a bad rep in forever affiliating them with wasteful consumption.

This is, of course, the Energy Vampire. That evil, electricity-and-income sucking entity that, because your juicing machine has been plugged into the outlet when you aren't using it, prohibits you from dressing properly for the Cannes Film Festival. What a wasteful race.

Despite its apparent prevalence in pretty much every household, to hear the Heat Meisters tell it, the term does not appear to be the household words the creative minds who give birth to such things might have promised. No doubt grateful are any real vampires who, otherwise suffering during a century of cinematic portrayal, clearly showed their thrift through their demonstrably clear Transylvanian translation of good-to-the-last-drop.

So, perhaps, in part, for reputational recompense to those slandered, spectral slayers, new words rise from the ashes now in an attempt to at least offer to even the score. And in so doing, this section of *Bereaveability* adopts these words to clarify its intent, something it has clearly not done with this and the above paragraphs.

Before you now, and unfortunately, all around you, is the Time Vampire.

Time Vampires are circling you practically every minute of every day. They are the people who directly and indirectly, through the application of idiocy and/or incompetence, literally suck away from you, for their own nefarious purposes, too-vast quantities of the limited time you have have left alive.

The devastating impact of this on your individual terminal timelines is not to be underestimated. This could be more effectively illustrated, for these purposes, should there be a reliable mathematical or other formula, algorithm or translation capable of converting seconds into wattage. The result would no doubt prove that Energy Vampires can't hold a candle to Time Vampires -- despite every toaster in America remaining sinfully plugged in, year-round. No, dwarfing that offensive electrical expenditure are those sucking out your living's livelihood with every tick of the clock.

Despite what mortgage companies and realtors would have you think, time is your single most important investment. You are given a chunk of it at birth, and it is largely up to you how you grow and extend it or mismanage or squander it. Given that you essentially house it, you may have more control over its location, location, location as you do its allocation.

Of course your overall time is subject to troubling market factors such as genetic demons and fatalistic interference. These can kick you pretty hard in your asset and bankrupt your portfolio, and very person, quicker than you can say "Damn, is that a 30-foot great white shark swimming this way?"

It must also be mentioned that Darwin's death did nothing to derail his discovery, although *survival of the fittest* has also undergone something of both a redefinition and a resurgence. Rather than dwelling on iguanas sequestered for centuries, and that are no doubt used to thinking "Why change, no one is coming over?," the popular, contemporary iteration tends to not show man at its finest.

In a nutshell, evolutionary observations have expanded to include the many remarkable bouts of intellectual dimness manifesting themselves as dangerous, if not lethal, actions and activities that threaten their very host by making them the target of the self-inflicted result. Unfortunately, sometimes they take others down with them.

Consequently, demonstrating abject stupidity resulting in the squandering or extinguishing of that subject's own time serves as the crucifix of crazy that keeps the truly voracious Time Vampires away and available to feed on those faster on the draw. Like the traditional vampire of Transylvanian fame in pursuit of a particularly gastronomically appealing blood type, those looking to waste your time by sucking it out of you only seem to do so if it has a correspondingly high value and succulence.

No Time Vampire nor traditional vampire wants to necessarily pursue a meal who's last words fall along the lines of " Man, the shade is nice here under that piano they're lowering from the 13th floor." or "I am lovin' this vacation. What a great day for an Amazonian piranha bath." Time Vampires fear the threat to themselves equal to the proximity to such hosts, and traditional vampires resent fate or fish sharing in their meal.

So, if you are swift(er) of mind, productive, efficient and resourceful in designing your life and all that you want to do with it, you are fair game.

The thing with time is that you own it, but really, you don't. Although you may have little control over losing it through some of life's expected expenditures such as wandering thoughts, prayer, porn, pleasure, passion and pissing, these are virtual nano-sections of your life's stockpile compared to the greater threats.

Time is taken from you by your job, your family, and by people you know and don't, of every possible description. When it is shared openly and voluntarily, the results can be met with disappointment. That is, what you offer by parting with yours seldom seems to give you the return you expected. And often, that's putting it mildly. Unfulfilling employment and chatty, wandering coworkers with too-clever coffee mugs are two of the most terrifyingly effective incarnations.

Not surprisingly, many of those who squander it most profligately are the first to complain that they never seem to have enough.

The point to all of this, of course, is the potential for mental torment through the added burden of clocking the reduction of your lifescore as it dissipates towards the mental entity, death, the younger versions of you refused to face. Are the most intolerant of time wasters also those who have begun to if not turn, at least peek around the corner on truly admitting the reality of their own demise? Could that be what makes them intolerant, resentful, even, ironically, homicidal, toward those who they perceive to be sucking that calendar creaminess out of their rapidly maturing middle? Probably.

All of this starts much sooner than you think.

The audible version of the angst of losing what little time you have may even be evident from birth, or possibly before, if shrieking babies are to be believed and until the reasons for such outcries are accurately translated. Maybe they already feel that with respect to time, they are already in the hole, a nascent and unpleasant thought as they are being forced by contraction into the one through which they entered, so much more romantically and easily much earlier.

Why cry? Why not? There you are being forcibly evicted from your wombular warmness and solace toward what, with its bright, overhead lighting, masked characters and efficient-looking machinery could easily be bank robbery in progress. All of this when the other of the two memories you have at this stage is entering into this entire proposition through Barry White and candlelight.

No, infantilistic time bombs don't gurgle, coo or sing from the birth canal, they cry and scream with whatever force they are able to muster given such limited lung capacity. It is possibly the first benchmark of belligerence, placing all within earshot on notice that they are not happy about these current developments related to their development.

And as happy with the idea of the arrival as post-expectant, placenta-plastered parents may be, they secretly and knowingly nod at that neonatal need for resistance. Many victims of hypnotists can apparently convey the pleasures of their uterine utopias -- breathing underwater while under ample breasts. What's not to like?

After losing the battle of the bulge, that mass that was the formerly safely ensconced you, and whether pushed, pulled or welcomed through a carefully carved custom entrance, the clock begins keeping score of the predations on your time. It is never again yours, and it will never seem to be enough. To consider you are lurching toward death from before you were born may be too much for too many to bear.

So well before you unilaterally convince yourself that potty training is absolutely unachievable, you develop sort of an I-won't-be-gypped-denial. Since frozen stopwatch time management in the *Twilight Zone* sense seem available to so few, the only other alternative is to ignore the end result. In that way, you are the master of your universe until your own, inevitable Bigish Bang of destruction which, of course, you won't see coming.

Assuming some kind of life begins at conception, which seems silly to dispute as long as the conversation isn't about ending it, your pre-natal clock is already set for leaps and bounds through the continuum. Your suggested gestation is conveniently quartered by months -- the progression of which are classified in the most scientifically meticulous terms: surprise, symptoms, girth and gifts. You are the baby in the proverbial bathwater, encapsulated, safe and warm, yet again, aging even before you are born.

After your debut at your blessed event, whether it be natural, induced, narcotically saturated, underwater, court ordered or unknown to your hostess until that horrific night at her Moon Dance-themed prom, the game is on. You've passed the first gauntlet, sliming through your afterbirth, after birth.

Then, everyday, ticking-based terminology defines the crime of time, albeit with blows softened over the centuries through harmless-sounding etymological adaptations. There is nap time, quiet time and playtime, for example, just three instances of how you are robbed simply because, in this case, the brain and body are pretty much nonambulatory and indefensible on their own.

Perhaps you had other plans -- and with people you much preferred over that big, wrinkled face with the thick glasses and that mole on her chin hovering over you like you are, sometimes for the second time, sitting in a petri dish. You are pretty clear that this in not your mother since you've never seen her with her shirt off and are sure, even at your age, that what little life you may have left might be best enjoyed if that situation remains unchanged.

Yet with age comes wisdom. Had your played your immediate post-natal cards differently then with whom you later realized was your wealthy Grammy-Nana, your inheritance might have been different today. Alas, shooting that urine fountain dead-on into her bloodshot orb during that diaper change seemed like the thing to do at the time. You'll show *them* how to put an eye out!

So years go by and it's off to bed, they clamor, at times completely conflicting with plans you made, and during which you need to be awake. Ironically, later, these same watchful wardens will espouse the importance of getting, what they instructively call, the-hell-out-of-bed.

Later, still, come the retrospective disciplinarily aberrations more frightening than the lyrics to "Rock a Bye Baby." These include passing the sentence of "time out" and that mystical and unsolvable mathematical aberration, "How many times have I told you...!?"

And with greater age brings greater awareness of the diabolical hold you are under. Rather than physically moving the blob that was you from one premeditated "beneficial" nurturing point of parental convenience, and back again, the directives now involve your active ambulatory acquiescence. In other words, in addition to the time-thievery, you are now physically endowed enough to march to your sentences. Tick. March. Tick. March. Tock.

When finally old enough to begin to even conceptualize the perceived value of one's own time, the development of a bargaining process is as much rude as wrong. But really, at this point, there is no other way. And frankly, you as the now experienced evaluator of the situation, know it.

From your teens into your 20s, you realize, more than ever, that anything resembling time with any kind of value, is now. Yet Vampires lurk in your own family. You are summarily and repeatedly charged with lifting and operating cleaning implements, propelling lawn-care-feeding-and-grooming machines and participating in the ceremonial bloodletting on the parental, and past-its-prime, crude-oiled carcass of the tribe's internal combustion engine.

These lessons one must learn. You suck it up because, as you are constantly reminded, your parents/guardians/foster folk OWN THE ROOF OVER YOUR HEAD and the air within it. Suck. And the knuckles busted and fingers split on crankshafts and oil pans are no longer kissed, coddled and Bactined. They are told to "man up," and you just want to hold a certain, bloodied finger up.

But with body hair, B.O. and bad attitudes begins the barking. Your time is attacked with such low blows as restrictive curfews -- that cleverly cleansed term used by the finest of sanctimonious familial households to describe keeping young, spontaneous boners from, usually only reluctant by nary a groin hair, young vaginal vortices. Usually. Oh, you know.

Regardless, it's a bad formula and a worse combination at a dangerous time. Capping hormones with curfew, many parents of teenagers will tell you, is like, well, when you were young, isn't it? Although you're feeling all adulty and authoritative now, parenthood also includes making the most of the not-so-little-one's time off of the premises to hide, erase, burn or bury any evidence from your misspent youth that in any way is likely to resemble theirs. Make fruitless your Red Bull-fueled Brandon's or Bethany's late-night snoop through your sock drawer while you're putting the Zzzzzzs in your La-Z-Boy. Set an example by destroying the evidence.

Depending upon your age, such an evidentiary trail may include: Sentimental (and usually scent-ridden) items, often hemp-related and from the Age of Aquarius through to the pre-meme of Madonna; diaries featuring sexual, pharmaceutical and/or felonious "experimentation" and/or evidence of out-of-town or out-of-the-country parental issue who were disenfranchised from your Norman Rockwell-ish Christmas/Hanukah/Kwanza mornings. How nice the holidays are unless you're the single parent progeny of an old girlfriend or an overseas war womb.

And it continues. The grandest theft of time for most, during one's 20s and 30s, becomes not only highway but diabolically self-inflicted: Romantic. This is the need for love or lust, of course. The mortality clock is still running, and that generation's generation of various, infatuation-produced fluids, male and female, seem to lubricate its gears. You give up more than your cherry. You enter into a long-term partnership with someone who helps design and perform ovarian or testicular topiary on your whole tree.

Where it goes from here depends on a number of things. If you're down with a higher power or fate showing more than a passing interest in when and how you will be passing, Vampires may mean less to you. Unless, of course, your higher power is a Vampire of the more traditional, nocturnal sort.

Or, is it all more scientific and the resulting from yet another of life's indecipherable algorithms -- cryptically imprinted into this land of lava and DNA even before we were microscopic, lapping dancers in the steaming pools and waves of earth's then predominant, prehistoric hot tubs? If it is indeed that complex, the Big Bang has a lot to answer for. Since eliciting such a response seems unlikely, probably the next worst thing is being given the intelligence, eventually, to come to some of your own conclusions which often include developing your own deadline denials.

13. POPI IS DEAD!

I can still see the signs. Literally, the signs. *"Popi is dead!"*

They were inartfully written and inartfully placed around my grandmother's house -- painfully and systematically by her daughters and son. They attempted to answer the question constantly posed by my increasingly forgetful grandmother, "Where is Popi?"

To a young mind devoid of anything resembling REAL mortality beyond dead goldfish and mail order lizards, and zero knowledge of mental illness, the main pain evident in my mother, aunts and uncle seemed borne of frustration. Yet it was frustration edged in an almost anger at having to constantly repeat to their 80-something mother that their father, her husband, had died 40 years earlier. An anger spawned by denial that, 40 years later, this author was also guilty of with his mother. How slowly everyone evolves.

You've heard it all before. The immigrant matriarch rock of the family, who came here from there with nothing and raised a brood of loving, middle-class-successful children who bred a generation economically and educationally above that -- and then who lost her connection with all that she brought forth out of that nothing. And they with her.

The intended audience for the signs was Busia (the deviant but phonetic and loving spelling we used for Polish grandmother). Busia was being subjected to these signs, written out of desperation by her unwaveringly devoted children. For them, hearing the person they respect and love calling out loud for a deceased person they also respected and loved is painful, stereophonically. After attempting to get through with reason through verbal explanation, no doubt in Polish and English, it's logical to think that a visual aid might work. The signs seemed to be everywhere. (Looking back, actually, there were probably only two. Curiously, they were in English, not in Busia's native Polish. But there was no doubt a reason for that.)

And as is the way, things only got worse. Having later been a front-line witness to the universal torture that is dementia with her daughter Josephine, this author's mother, there were phases. And paradoxically, some were a relief.

In this severely demented state, whether one calls or diagnoses it as Alzheimer's Disease or something else, for some it protects the mind of the one it infects. What could be a disease that triggers all of the blames and horrors of one's life often seems to let up -- to allow the channels that open and begin to function in some new way to instead focus on childhoods and pleasant pasts -- pasts often unknown to the sibling or offspring or even the spouse who now cares for them.

For the victim, there is still some anxiety and worry, often for that mysterious, lost friend, unknown sibling or even lover. Busia's was Gabrisha, also the subject of countless inquiries and a past ghost to us all, a soul never to to known to anyone but her. Whoever she was, she was clearly at one point a comfort to Busia, a fact that made it all the more agonizingly painful to those in the family who could not produce her.

But mercifully abated is this terror was the echoing of every pain they've had or mistake they've made -- demons so easily available to be constantly drummed into an otherwise helpless mind. Frankly, that's often the burden of the "sane," everyone else, and what the lucid living live with. Denial is just one of the reliable mechanisms available to be drawn upon to block such horrors.

And maybe, secretly, that's why you don't fight the invitation into this mellow morass when you are invited -- that place where you give up our thoughts to anyone or anything else because you don't know what to do with them anymore. You do this even if you can somehow still grasp that you become a lesser you. Maybe everyone on this path is just tired, and dementia knows when that when is. And it comes. And you let it in. And you go.

But like that secret invitation to a Top Secret club, you can't tell anyone upon its approach, or don't want to, for fear of...oh, you don't remember. It just doesn't seem right to push your mind so much more after it has worked so hard for so long. Could your one, last, truly sound assessment of our own mental capabilities be used to weigh the privileges of abandoning them?

As this all envelopes you, perhaps even earlier than you would like to admit, with pride and independence and all, do you ultimately care less about the ramifications to those who care about you and what they will do with your body during the transition? You may wonder, but maybe your planning about such things is ending. Maybe it should. Maybe you've done enough. Enough!

Some may believe Busia died never re-remembering what happened to Popi. But I suspect she already knew. Her children, those now gone, now know, if there is an afterlife or an afterdeath.

But, after her having attended his funeral and to his affairs 40 years before, was that really her question? Perhaps she was afraid of where she was going, and she didn't want to go alone. Perhaps her question wasn't "Where is my husband, why isn't he next to me now in my living life?" but rather, "I am going to someplace foreign, again, and why isn't he with me for this journey, to help with our new home? Will he be there when I get there?"

I suspect the latter, wherever that is. Wherever everyone goes. Not because it's easier and less painful to think about it that way, but because I know.